BEAT SCRAPBOOK

"These poems in Gerald Nicosia's *BEAT SCRAPBOOK* are like old snapshots of familiar faces and places you may or may not remember, but the details and the depth and the angles and the framing are so compellingly poignant and resonant you feel it's yourself he's capturing in words, which are the melody to the songs of ourselves."

— Michael Lally

"If you want a rolling, rollicking history of poetry, poets, and life from the '60's till now, take a trip through Gerald Nicosia's *Beat Scrapbook*. Through his eyes we get an appreciation for the bubbling creativity that was everywhere if you knew where to look, as he surely did."

— Joanna McClure

"Empathy for others, especially those with troubled lives—in short, *love*—seems to be the force that through the red veins drives Nicosia's poetry flowers. They're *peopled* like the poems of no other writer I'm familiar with these days. Real, specific people. It's like I can reach out and touch them, because he has reached out and touched me."

— Chuck Brickley

BEAT SCRAPBOOK

Gerald Nicosia

Introduction by Michael Schumacher

Coolgrove Press

Coolgrove Press, an imprint of
Cool Grove Publishing, Inc. New York.
512 Argyle Road, Brooklyn, NY 11218
All rights reserved under the International and
Pan-American Copyright Conventions.
www. coolgrove. com
For permissions and other inquiries write to
info@coolgrove. com

ISBN: 978-1887276-36-8
Library of Congress catalog number applied for.

The author wishes to extend his gratitude to the editors
of the publications where many of these poems first
appeared:

*Soft Need 23, The New York Quarterly, Literary Hub, Black Ace,
Maintenant, House Organ, Blue Beat Jacket, Beatitude Gold-
en Anniversary Anthology, (Ed Coletti's) NO MONEY IN PO-
ETRY, The End Is the Beginning, Sick Fly, Specious Species,
CER*BER*US, ZZZ ZYNE, POEMS-FOR-ALL No. 135, Marin
Poetry Center Anthology Volume Eight, Poetry Flash, MillVal-
leyLit, Last Call: The Bukowski Legacy Continues, Pitchfork,*
and *The Scribbler*

Coolgrove Press is a past recipient of
Community of Literary Magazines and Presses **[CLMP]**'s
Face Out Re-grant funded by
the Jerome Foundation.

This book is distributed to the trade by **SPDBooks**

Media alchemy by Kiku

Coolgrove Press

to my grandparents
Joseph "Little Joe" and Anna Fremer
Calogero and Alfonsa Nicosia
and
to my parents
Peter and Sylvia Nicosia

Table of Contents

Other Books by Gerald Nicosia

Bughouse Blues

Memory Babe: A Critical Biography of Jack Kerouac

The Two Lowells of Jack Kerouac

Lunatics, Lovers, Poets, Vets & Bargirls (poetry)

Home to War: A History of the Vietnam Veterans' Movement

Love, California Style (poetry)

Embrace of the Lepers (poetry)

Jan Kerouac: A Life in Memory

One and Only: The Untold Story of On the Road

Night Train to Shanghai (poetry)

The Last Days of Jan Kerouac

The Ghost of Kerouac (poetry)

Kerouac: The Last Quarter Century

INTRODUCTION

Poets, it seems to me, are tellers of secrets. The best poets find unique ways of offering us secrets within the familiar. We find aspects of our lives and thoughts buried in the lines. We'll read a finely crafted poem and, upon reflecting on it, we'll say, "Oh, so that's what that's all about." Or something similar. It's the clarity of the thought or symbol that matters.

I had these thoughts when reading *Night Train to Shanghai*, Gerald Nicosia's collection of poems addressing his journeys to China. I had never been to China, but after encountering Nicosia's observations about the country, I felt as if I had. Further, he delivered work that unlocked some of my own thoughts, hidden away or unrealized, in a way that seemed honest and true.

I wondered about this again when I began *Beat Scrapbook*. I have studied the Beat Generation for a half-century. I've read the writings. I've read the biographies, memoirs, and correspondence. What could he write that I didn't already know?

The answer is plenty.

Nicosia established his credentials in Beat scholarship a long time ago. His *Memory Babe*, published in 1983, remains the high-water mark in the line of Kerouac biographies. *Jan Kerouac: A Life in Memory* and *One and Only*, the story of Lu Anne Henderson, a major figure in *On the Road*, addressed two figures that deserved better than footnote status in a male-dominated Beat canon. Most recently, in *Kerouac: The Last Quarter Century*, Nicosia turned a critical eye on the desecration of Kerouac's estate and literary legacy in a tale so perverse that it would seem the stuff of imagination if documentation wasn't provided. Then there's the Beat-related prose and poetry that Nicosia published in newspapers and magazines.

While assembling this bibliography of notable work, Nicosia met, interviewed, corresponded with, and, in many cases, established friendships with a whole array of Beat Generation figures, and this personal relationship with the Beats informs the poetry in this volume. It also influences the direction some of the poems take.

Nicosia is a purveyor of detail. In his prose, he sprinkles details judiciously, a chef including spices, however sparingly, to design a creation his own. In his poetry, a single detail can become the point of the poem. This is exceedingly important in brief portraits, in which one or two details spell the difference between clear understanding and vague notion.

A poem such as "The Atom Bomb of Genius" stands out because Nicosia attempts a brief characterization of someone—in this case, Gregory Corso—in a way that catches the essence of complexity in few words. It was never a good idea to understand Corso too easily, but it was important to see his many sides. He was, perhaps more than any member of the Beat Generation, the personification of "beat." He was scruffy, endearing, rude, largely self-educated, brilliant, maddening. That was the improbability of Corso: he was sweet yet infuriating.

Nicosia, who devotes two poems to Corso, absolutely nails it with just a few lines:

> the most outstanding thing about you
> was your undaunted, unfazed
> unstoppable originality

Or this, a fragment about Kerouac, telling you all you need to know about his love of Lowell, Massachusetts and the years of his youth:

> . . . the leaves are drifting through the early dark of October
> And the poor teenage school kids are hurrying home
> Past the eternal drugstores and cheap food places
> On ancient cobbled Merrimack Street

And the damp air of fall gets in my bones
And the smell of car exhausts rises and
Disappears in the low grey murk
Of Massachusetts heaven
I think of you Jack

Sometimes, when reading Nicosia's poetic scrapbook, you feel as if you are at a parade, standing curbside, watching familiar faces walk by, each poet a sparkle in a mosaic picturing a history that cannot be overlooked or forgotten. Lawrence Ferlinghetti appears in a tribute commemorating his hundredth birthday. Richard Brautigan, the quirky poet, novelist, and short fiction writer, is the focus of two poems contrasting his warmth and humor with his tragic, self-inflicted end. Jan Kerouac, recipient of the full treatment in another Nicosia book, shines in a light denied her in life. Her famous father, as one might expect, is depicted for his creative genius and deep sadness that couldn't be anesthetized by an army of boilermakers. There are poems constructed around Ted Joans' grocery list and George Dowden's lying, unnoticed, in Walt Whitman's bed.

But this is not a book with thoughts turned to only the famous or nearly famous Beats. Nicosia strides in and out of these pages, his personal entries, most notably of his relationship with his father, adding texture to his depictions of the Beats. There's an unsettling commentary on Death Row. Singer/songwriter Steve Goodman appears, unannounced yet totally appreciated, at Nicosia's front door. Years of memories, stripped down to minimalism, are stark sentinels, silhouetted against the backdrop of a consciousness now prepared to share them with strangers.

And we, as readers, are gifted with both familiarity and surprise.

–Michael Schumacher
Author of *Dharma Lion: A Biography of Allen Ginsberg*

Gerald Nicosia

THE BEAT FATHER OF CHICAGO POETRY

Paul Carroll was a drinker

And a kind man

We split many a bottle of wine

And in my mind's eye whenever

I recall him I see a half-empty bottle of Roditis

On the table in front of us

In a noisy narrow crowded restaurant

In Chicago's Greek Town

And Paul is smiling

Always smiling as he always

Pours the wine into my glass

Before his

There was nothing this man wanted

More than the company of those

Who liked him and his poetry

And from that gentle need

He created a whole world of Chicago literature

And a community of writers

Who learned to give more than they took

The Circle Campus Writing Program

The Poetry Center

Big Table Press

He spun out an array of beautiful clothes

For every poet and writer in Chicago to wear

For all of us in this city had been naked

Or near naked since

The city burned down

And we all grew up so hard, naked in the cold

That we didn't know how hard our life was

Till Paul Carroll brought us warm and beautiful clothes

And rose-colored wine to drink

And the poets and writers of Chicago

Got so drunk on that wine

They forgot who had brought it to them

They forgot the Beat Father of Chicago Poetry

As they went on to their various successes

They forgot that he had written it all a thousand times better

Before any of them had touched pen to paper

They did not honor him

And his last bottle of Roditis emptied

But he still kept smiling

And walked away from the table

To a land called North Carolina

And wrote us all letters

On ruled yellow legal paper

To keep us strong and remembering

All the great poets before and after him

That his life stood

As a permanent tribute to

And his death

Will transform into

Seeds of endless rebirth.

POEM ON SEEING AND HEARING GARY SNYDER AT ALMOST 90 AT THE MILL VALLEY LIBRARY

for Jack Kerouac, "Memory Babe"

There are deer and there are hawks but there

Is only one Gary Snyder

You want me to love the wild

But I love you, Gary

Because there is only one of you

And you will soon be

Extinct

Gary Snyder champion of the wild

And lover and defender of the earth

Walked through that crowd of several hundred people

At the Mill Valley Library

Looking stooped and shrunken

And oh so vulnerable

Coughing from deep in his chest

As he took the mike

And held us spellbound

For over an hour

With all the things that have

Fascinated him for nine decades

Who else but this one man

Loves ancient Chinese characters

Japanese haiku

Australian wildfires

And can also brag that

For a single year of earth-time,

In the confused and turbulent 1950's,

He was Jack Kerouac's best friend?

Gary comes to us as a teacher

But I'm not sure I learned anything

I didn't already know

At least from his talk that night at the library

But I'll never forget the unique

Dazzling combination

Of his sparkling eyes

Wiry, itchy, energetic frame

(even at almost 90!)

Fast, soft, throaty voice

Filled with enthusiasm for life

In all its forms

And the things life teaches

And especially the wild chuckle that keeps erupting

From the deepest, wildest, craziest part of him

That has remained untamed and untameable

For almost ninety years

He's merry, angry, cranky, smart

Sly and tricky as Coyote

And he'll never fall in anybody's trap

Or be anyone's pet animal

His memories are his trail

And he lets us walk it with him

For a little while that night

At the almost century-old Mill Valley Library

Which somebody built well

He reminds us

As your words flow over us

I'm standing right there with you

On Grant Avenue in North Beach

In the vanished pivotal moment of 1958

When under a streetlight Robert Duncan's crossed eyes

Gleam madly as he

Signs the very first copy of his book *Letters*

For you

A moment that is now eternal

Though it was gone in less than a second

Duncan, Rexroth, Spicer, long dead

Live for us again

As you tell of them

Arguing fiercely with one another

About poetry

No blood was spilled

But the hot intellectual life of the 1950's

Spilled all over the streets and pads of a gone world

Spilled all over you

And live on now only

In your crowded brain

And fecund river of words

That we are privileged to hear

Once only ourselves

And then will be gone in an instant

Like the Temple of Jerusalem

Except in our own living memories

Of this momentous, vanished night—

You tell of these men arguing with

Furious passion

And yet still loving each other

In a way that has been lost and buried

In the sands of time

Or buried as the treasures of Venice will be

Someday under the floods

Of global warming

And only your reaching a hand down

(or up)

To pull them into our sight once more

For a flashing instant

Can defeat oblivion

But you can do this only

Because you are Gary Snyder

And all the magnificent black bear and redtailed hawks

In the world

Cannot do this without

Your endangered self which

As you say

Will soon be no more

Yes, we can save all the wild animals

And plants in the world

And we should save them

If we can

But we need also to save

Every single precious human being

And the precious memories

They carry with them

Or there will be nothing left

Anywhere in the universe

Worth saving

Gerald Nicosia

Like this radiant star

Named Gary Snyder

With us for only a

Nonexistent ninety or so years

And then, like waking from a dream

No longer there

Except as a memory

For it's of memories like these

The universe is made.

THE MAN NO ONE HATED

to the memory of Bob Kaufman (1925-1986)

Bob, it's 18 years since we met,

you looking raggedy-taggedy

but with jaunty beret and serape

stumbling, falling forward

as you always did

across Broadway and Columbus

me yelling out,

"Are you Bob Kaufman?"

and you answering without hesitation,

eyes awake and curious,

"Yes!"

8 years now since you died

when I was out of town

and I didn't get to see your jazz funeral

up Columbus

and the scattering of your ashes

off Angel Island

to create one of the best

rainbows of the year.

Besides the fact that you

were the truest saint I knew,

least concerned with material things,

there's still this one great shining beauty—

that no one hated you

maybe because you laid claim

to nothing

except our hearts

and even then made better than fair trade

with your own.

FERLINGHETTI

Lawrence never let me treat him like a famous man
I sat down to interview him
a green 27-year-old Midwestern kid
He said, "You need a better microphone than that"
I said, "I don't know where to get one"
He said, "C'mon, I'll take you"
And he led me six blocks away
to an electronics store
and showed me which one to buy
When Jan Kerouac was in town
and shy of celebrity herself
Lawrence said, "Bring her to my house
to meet Paula and we'll have coffee"
I can't remember what we talked of that day
but I can still see Jan's smiling and laughing face
in that well-worn house on Francisco
filled with old wood and books
He relaxed Jan as
he relaxes everyone

That's one of his trade secrets

but it's also real

and that's another one of his secrets

I remember having breakfast with him and my mom

in a little café

on the Rue St. Louis in old Quebec

during the *Rencontre Internationale Jack Kerouac*

and how he delighted my old mother

with jokes about the real maple syrup

and stories he remembered of her

hometown Chicago

She told me afterward

"I liked the way his eyes twinkled when he talked"

And I remember his earnestness when he told

Stella Kerouac in

the old Pollard Library in Lowell

that she had to let him publish

Jack's manuscript *Pomes All Sizes*

and didn't falter under her Greek anger

because he knew he was in the right

And I remember him telling me

with a grim face

in the offices of City Lights

during the first Gulf War

that it was time for poets to end their silence
and speak up about things that matter
"I'm still waiting," he said,
and God bless him,
he's still waiting now,
a hundred years after his birth,
and it's high time
we gave him what he asked for.

SCRAPBOOKS

The old poets gather in Vesuvio's
talking and taking pictures of each other
studying the old photos on the wall
and remembering people who are dead
or who will never again look
as they did when
they stared into the little black hole
that preserves ghosts
the best way we've yet invented
the spirits of their friends are all around them
Wieners has just died
before that it was Kesey,
before him, Corso,
before Corso, Micheline
they stare back into the past like
a chain of graves
then glance out the window
all strangers walking by
not even a friendly face in City Lights
wondering what happened to human kindness

to friendly publishers

to fights for justice on the barricades

and to a public that revered the written word

it's all just a smile in the camera

it will all be remembered by someone

in a book or

in a library archive

who will think it all made sense

once upon a time

and the poets smile because they know

that once upon a time

it did.

Gerald Nicosia

THE THREE BLOODED BROTHERS[*]

for Tony Scibella (1932-2003)

Voice of war, voice of peace

Your majestic profile cut across

My workspace every day in

The broadside photo given me by

Jimmy long ago up in his mountain hideout

With him and Stu standing as if

Protective over you &

Stu's deathly powerful poem "moonwash sea"

Which left no doubt you guys

Were in it for life together

And not giving an inch to

Popularity or social demands—

What I remember most now

Besides sorrow at never having got to meet

Your living human fireball

Was yr kindness to me in letters

Late in the game when

You could have opted to play

Solitary successful highhat

But wrote me instead like Italian father

Concerned that I carry it on—

Hope you dig death.

*The "three blooded brothers" were Tony Scibella, James Ryan Morris, and Stuart Z. Perkoff.

Gerald Nicosia

POEM FOR MY HAITIAN FRIEND AND
THE SNOWS OF YESTERYEAR

Eugene, old bartender friend,

someday when you walk past Java coffeeshop

which isn't Java any more

but high-tech vegan restaurant

$40 a plate and "keep moving"

will you remember me,

shy bearded poet,

sitting at far table over $1 coffee

so many early afternoons

just back from visiting my mom in nursing home,

reading or scribbling or taking notes,

then out into the sunlight or rain

to go home and work some more

bothering no one

except for a spoon or some half and half?

Eugene, will you have a pleasant thought of me

in years that have long-since disappeared

just as myself passing the house where I grew up

4143 Custer Avenue, Lyons, Illinois

(my return address for 30 years)

wished I could see the four-year-old

boy in cowboy hat inside

watching *Lone Ranger, Howdy Doody*, or *Cinnamon Bear*

who would someday grow into writer me

with two parents and half a lifetime of experience

buried forever in a mind

that won't forget

and remains forever at war

with the world that takes away?

Gerald Nicosia

IN MEMORIAM JAN KEROUAC

Jan, we walked together down Lower East Side streets
almost got run over by a few cabs
you got angry at me dawdling and dreaming
in the middle of New York streets
You can't do that in New York, she said
I can if I'm a philosopher, I said
Yeah, and you'll get killed, she said
Maybe I don't care, I said
Aw, man you're weird! she mocked
in raunchiest New York accent
but she liked playing mother to me
and everyone around her
maybe because no mother or father most of the time
in her own life
teaching people how to cook apple pie the proper way
"Actually more of an English pie than American"
she lectured Stanley and Lil out in Northport
our nostrils filled with cinnamon and melted sugar
as we all eagerly awaited the fruits
of her baking

Jan was a lover of people

a loner and unloved herself

who always had a gift for everyone

didn't care that her own purse

was mostly empty

her bedroom full of luscious clothes

but no one to model them for

at the end she kept leaving herself notes

and when her eyes got bad

she wrote on a chalkboard

"Remember to buy TV dinners" she'd write

and still forget to buy them

but the nurses at the hospital fed her for free

and she died full

of the admiration and respect

of more than a few of us

who still care about her.

Gerald Nicosia

THE GHOST OF KEROUAC

Every time I walk the streets of Lowell

And the leaves are drifting through the early dark of October

And the poor teenage school kids are hurrying home

Past the eternal drugstores and cheap food places

On ancient cobbled Merrimack Street

And the damp air of fall gets in my bones

And the smell of car exhausts rises and

Disappears in the low grey murk

Of Massachusetts heaven

I think of you Jack

It's like you're walking with me

Listening to my woes

And telling me your own

Pulling your jacket tighter to keep out the chill

Your eyes with that far-away look

Like a veteran's thousand-yard stare

You saw the future even before you died

And that's why you always looked so sad

It's so hard to care, you said

For people who are going to die

And then *you* did

But it didn't keep you from coming back

A thousand nights

A thousand times a thousand nights

They can't keep you out of Lowell

Because even ghosts

Have to have a home

And yours is with the lonely wakeful spirit

Of man

And woman

Wherever it's found

And this town will always be

A lonely flame

In the pained human heart

Of poverty and misery

And everyday suffering

And as long as there's a human heart left

To care about that

You'll still be here

Among us

To keep us company

On life's broken road.

Gerald Nicosia

THIS IS YOUR LIFE
to Charmaine

Born illegitimate under a Hawaiian sun
that kept burning black-hot under your skin
despite the problems
the endless problems
you turned up at twenty
in a Long Beach hospital
suffering from ulcers
and a murdered heart
I found you later in a singles bar
on Fillmore Street in San Francisco
playing dice games with the bartender
to keep from getting drunk
I used to wonder how you did it
how you even managed to get up on time
after an all-night riot that would have put
the Corybants to shame
all those little tricks you had with the alarm
and pushing the minute hand ahead
and how you never failed to find the clothes

you'd strewn across the living room the night before

the rapid sea-change in the bathroom

the thundering shower and a little makeup

clearing off the sweat of sleep

the salt that was so good to taste on waking

on the back of your neck

and the burnt-earth smell of your hair

transformed into a dripping mop

above your cheerful smile, flashing eyes

and fast walk to the bus stop

raging always but never questioning

what had to be done

this life you'd been given such an utter mess

I'd never have accepted it

as readily or totally as you

you talked of suicide but only

as I later understood

to let off steam, release the stress

that might have really led to it

you loafed at work

but never have I known so hard a worker

at the job of straightening out the bends

of God or nature or whoever made you hurt so bad

whoever put those nerve-ends in your soul

that register the earthquake

of every cruel abrasion

you knew how many things you needed

you didn't want to use me

you used me anyway and I was glad

to be a station on so long a journey

as if you were a famous spiritual athlete

a Marco Polo of deliverance

who had all Asia to traverse

just to get a good night's sleep.

THE HEART GOES ON:
POEM WRITTEN AT THE MILL VALLEY BOOK DEPOT

for Joe Donohoe

Dreaming of Jack London

Kerouac walked down Miller Avenue

To his date with Gary Snyder

And destiny

Kerouac has vanished

Like the "painted-up Buddha doll"

That Ginsberg called him

But *The Dharma Bums*

Is a great book

The same rain is falling now

As then

"Lust and rage" still

"dance attendance" on the old age

Of a new generation

All the trappings fall away

The old books and manuscripts

Disintegrate

Young beauties grow old

And die

The Human Heart

Goes on

And only those who speak

For the Human Heart

Endure.

FOURTH OF JULY WITH THE BUK IN SAN PEDRO

for Charles Bukowski

He stands in a cheap plaid shirt
like some long-forgotten comedian
eyeing me sidewise
wondering what I want out of him
amazed that he's still alive
after 70 years of people coming at him
pleased by the magic he's still got
that keeps making books upstairs
on his little Mac computer
with the ancient radio blaring
the best classical music
after a day at the track
in one of the best Jap cars
money can buy
so many people coming to visit
the millionaire writer
in his fancy home and lush green yard
with self-cleaning swimming pool

don't see the lonely, troubled man

still inside

70 years haven't blunted the pain

of getting out of bed every morning

with an ugly face and a treacherous body

the horror of boredom

and the ever-nearing grave

they want to make him a hero

of the lost and down-and-out

king of the losers

what a joke

losers don't have kings

and Buk almost stumbles and falls

into the outdoor cooking grill

with wife Linda rushing to save him

though he'd already gotten his balance back

despite the dozen beers already downed

he plays with it all

the joke of holidays

celebrating your nation's independence

when your nation never gave you anything

but a big kick in the ass

and most of all the guests he invited

unaware they're foils for his madness

his need to compose their needs and hopes

into story after story

using humanity like notes in a symphony

it makes him happier than booze

and he can't figure out why

life can still be this good

when it's also so awfully

awfully bad.

Gerald Nicosia

WHAT I'M HIDING FROM
(OR: WHY I LIVE IN CALIFORNIA)

for Kaviraj George Dowden

I'm hiding from people like you, George

Who want to know the color of my soul's underwear

And whether there's fire in my brainstem

Or if I can crack poetry nuts without

A Norton's nutcracker

I'm afraid to tell them

How many times I can come in one night

Because this earth is a dangerous place

To tell people anything

They can stamp a number on

And the truth is I

Sometimes write poems

To keep the world away

But most of the time

It's really a coded map

To let the seekers like yourself

Find what's left of me.

FOR JACK

to the memory of my dear friend Jack Micheline (1929-1998)

Jack, you were an ornery cuss

I watched you piss off more people than I could count

saw you yell at even gutsy Ron Kovic

when he stole your audience

by reading his own stuff on the sidewalk

outside your reading

you didn't take shit from no one Jack

and yet you were full of love too

you loved even those who hated you

but loved most the poor, the lost,

the ones for whom no one else cared

the "fat girls on the bus" you used to talk of—

"they need love more than anyone," you said

and of course the feminists hated you

for saying it,

you were sexist, chauvinist, anti-business

on the wrong side of everybody's tracks

the most politically incorrect person

this side of Rush Limbaugh

but I swear I hardly ever knew anyone

with a bigger heart

or anyone who felt more the pain and beauty

of this strange experience we call life

I watched you blow countless audiences away

even the tough young punks on Broadway

who came to ridicule

and walked away amazed and wondering at your power

to speak the world they lived in

many decades after you came into it

I watched you win literary prizes

like Kesey awarding you "best performance"

at Naropa in 1982 when you made all those superstars

like Burroughs, Waldman, Hoffman, and Ginsberg

pale beside your booming cuss at America

and everybody who went thru life

with their eyes shut

Jack you taught me so much

how to see, how to listen, how to learn from the street

like a garden of rare, beautiful flowers

no one too small, too poor, too insignificant

for your golden attention

Jack, I can't do you justice in this poem

I had the honor of having walked with you

and listened to your wisdom

and felt the touch of your tender eyes on mine

your eyes so special, so full of hurt and understanding

when they weren't aflame with rage

at the injustices of society

capitalism, and the publishing biz

Like Whitman you sang the joy of the body, of "spade kicks"

sex and food and booze and pretty girls

you understood Kerouac's daffiness

and wandered the same lonely path of misunderstood genius

you gave me some paintings I'll always cherish

and fifteen pounds of xeroxed manuscripts

that no one would publish

I gave you a ride home from a lonely party in Berkeley

one rainy night when no one else would take you

you told me it was a "mitzvah"

a blessing that would come for helping you

the "mitzvah" was your friendship, Jack

a million memories of one totally unique being

named Harvey Martin Silver Jack Micheline
ragged lion of the streets
and giant of kindness
whose ear was a perennial post office box
that no one will ever replace.

POEM FOR TWO GREAT AMERICAN POETS

George Dowden climbed into

Walt Whitman's bed in New Jersey

when the docent was downstairs

and couldn't see

George's moment of private fame

lasted only a second or two

but his life was changed by his

communion with

the greatest poet in the world

he believed

George said, if you don't write like Whitman

you might as well quit poetry

he didn't mean you had to write

another "Song of the Open Road"

or "Calamus"

But that you had to see America with eyes

that looked through a country

to the stars a million light years

away, and feel your own

sweating flesh at the same time

and still be able to

jump out of the bed

and look innocent

by the time the docent

came back upstairs.

FOR JACK KEROUAC IN NORTHPORT

I stood in the middle of Main Street

in the black, wet air

of Northport night

with those old streetcar tracks

still stuck in the concrete road

in front of Gunther's Bar

where you laid down one night

after the bars had closed

when the cars were all pulling out

the young kids getting set to drag race

their headlights glaring over your body

nearly invisible in the shadows

while you invited your own death

till Stanley joked you

back to your feet

and out of harm's way

temporarily

last night the cars

were pulling out again

you could hear the gulls in

the harbor

and the happy revelers chattering

and laughing

as you must have heard

them that night

watching Stanley toddle drunkenly

back to his studio

and thinking about your lonely

house back up on the hill

with widowed mother and too many cats

for a moment I was you

and I felt how hard that choice

must have been

standing there all by yourself

apart from the happy world

no one to tell you

which way to go

then I saw you

still on your own

after taking a few beats

turn and

with furrowed brow

go home to Mémère

and literary history.

LENORE

for Lenore Kandel

Lenore

Smiling

Gentle

Keeping her genius quiet

So that only a few knew

Her heart large

Her suffering long

Her patience endless

Her love unbreakable

Could never say no

Must have embraced death

Like a lover

My only sadness

That the new joys she's found

Will never be told

To us

In yet another poem.

Gerald Nicosia

POEM FOR JACK MUELLER (1942-2017)

What I remember most—your cigarettes and your
    bourbon
and the crazy gleam in your eye when you got a
    new idea
you were a fountain, a machine of ideas
had a hard time making them real
which you knew, but no one cared
we wanted too much that magic you
gave out as freely as the poems or the jokes
you'd recite for anyone anywhere who
took the time to listen to you
in that deep, resonant voice
that could have come out of a Kentucky coal mine
if coal miners had all the wisdom of the ages
at the tip of their tongue
You were one of a kind, "Don't include me
with all those Jacks!" you'd say
in your mock-angry voice—or maybe
it was real anger too
for sure it was real compassion you had
for almost all of us, for me I know
you truly worried about

how vulnerable I was to women and you

told me once, "Don't let Charmaine

make you her ponce!"

and who else but Jack Mueller

could say it in just that way?

you loved your daughter terribly

"There's nothing better in the world,"

you told me, "than reading

"the Sunday comics with her, the paper all

spread out and both of us

on our knees, laughing

our heads off!"—you didn't believe in God

but if that wasn't a kind of praying

I don't know what is.

I dreamed of you four months before you died

I'd never dreamed of you before in 40 years

You were in some kind of danger,

a train was coming

I tried to reach you but couldn't get your number

I'm writing this poem because

it's the only way I have

of reaching you now.

SMALL POEM FOR RICHARD BRAUTIGAN

for Georgina

Last night at the Book Shop Santa Cruz
They asked me to sign a book
For someone I hadn't met
I signed with love and affection
Just as I've written so many poems
For you
With love and affection
Whom I've also never met
I'm not going to end this poem
With a corny line about us
Meeting in heaven
Because the fact is
We've already met through your words
Just like the anonymous book buyer
Will meet me
When they ship off my signed book
Words are the best way to meet anyway
They've always beaten bodies
Thank God we're writers
No?

THE POET AS PROTEUS

for David Meltzer

Every time I see him he's someone different

sometimes he's a merry red-faced

George Burns with a cane

sometimes an aging cowpoke

in faded jeans and ten-gallon hat

sometimes a minor movie star

eyes hidden behind shades

nothing visible but huge moustache

and sly smile

not giving a damn about Academy Awards night

he'd rather spend the night

alone writing another poem in

those endless small cheap notebooks

he's been filling for over fifty years

with his humorously disguised

stiletto intelligence

I remember him as the minister

at Jack Hirschman's wedding

giving a sermon about "Alpha and Omega"

that no one could understand

least of all frowning Hirschman

waiting to grab and kiss his new wife

he's also been my serious and optimistic

literary advisor on numerous occasions

he always turns up like

an angel or

the bearer of a mitzvah

just when I most need him

like the ABA in Los Angeles in '94

when my big book on veterans

had been orphaned and he

pointed me toward the next publisher

I've always loved the fact that

he scorns anyone making

poetry for money

but he gives a kind nudge

not a slap when he

sees me or anyone else

slipping a bit off

the altruistic path

no one funnier to listen to

even at almost 70

no poet sexier to the ladies

he carries his greatness

lightly like a shawl

of memories, joys, and

sadnesses

always with him

but hardly noticeable

until he takes it off

and asks you to

hold it for him

awhile

and you feel its enormous weight

and wonder how

he has worn it so long

with that perpetual

soft easygoing cheerfulness

that will be the mark

he leaves on all of us

whether we

read his poetry or not

and he doesn't care

if we read it or not

the joy is

in the making

and he doesn't sell

that secret

like most great writers

but gives it

not even for the asking

but just along with

the grace of

his company

to those

lucky enough

to find it.

THE GHOST OF BILL BURROUGHS

Having lunch with Harold Norse at Max's

fragile, grey, 82-year-old friend

and almost father

who's impeccably dressed—

sportcoat, vest, striped shirt

like a businessman

but black-and-yellow checked wool scarf

of a poet

we talk of old friends, Bill Burroughs,

"He loved me," Harold says

and so much is there in the noisy

modern, yuppie, neon-lit, glass-clinking restaurant

with us—

a whole lifetime of literary experience

behind him

years at the Beat Hotel in Paris

stories that will never be told.

"Brion Gysin was a big man, loud voice,

and completely captivating

ninety-nine percent of the time he was warm and friendly

but when he was angry
he'd turn stone cold."
A white light shines from Harold's face
uplifting me
with his love of the world and people
his kindness toward existence
never conquered
by its unkindness toward him.
Behind him, as if from nowhere,
a tall old man appears
sitting at the bar
awaiting his table
hunched over his shiny mahogany cane
iron grey receding hair slicked back
elegant dark-blue Brooks Brothers suit
too big on his shrinking frame
and when he turns full face to me
I exclaim to Harold,
"It's Bill Burroughs! By God!
Is this synchronicity, or what?"
Harold looks at the man,
nods,
then back at me with sly smile
"It happens to me all the time—

been happening all my life."
And just as suddenly, sadly,
I wonder, *will Harold appear*
to me like that someday
when he too's no longer
really here?
and where will I be then?
several years closer to my own ghosthood?
I walk Harold, now grown so slow and delicate
back to my car
and put him safely in,
leaving the noisy, crowded Civic Center behind
for the short ride
back to his lonely, dark home
in the Mission
filled with shelves of dusty books
stacks of dusty manuscripts
and ghosts I don't even know.

Gerald Nicosia

POEM FOR GREGORY CORSO'S ASHES
IN THE ENGLISH CEMETERY IN ROME

Dear Gregory, as long as I knew you

They were throwing you out of places

I watched Bob Levy

Normally a kind man

Give you the bum's rush out of City Lights

Yelling, "We want your books here

But not you!"

(There was a rumor you'd broken in one night

And rifled the cash register

For the royalties they forgot to pay you

But you couldn't prove it

By me.)

I saw your name in concrete outside Vesuvio's

Meaning you were permanently eighty-sixed

For going up to a cute woman and

Telling her, with an impish grin

"I'd like to eat your cunt!"

One night at Dante's Bar

(how ironic)

When you'd gotten a little rambunctious

They again threatened to toss you out

And you told them that if they did

You'd come back with "a *pistola* . . .

A Roscoe," and teach them a lesson

The barkeep threatened back,

"We got plenty of *pistole* of our own"

And you told him, "You dummy,

I'm not talking about a real gun,

I'm talking about the hot lead

In my mind!"

Now I hear they're about to evict

Your ashes

From the English Cemetery in Rome

Where I sat on your marble tombstone

And played with the feral cats

Who came by all day long to

Pay homage

To your catlike grace

They say you're not paying

Your rental bill

For the cemetery plot

On time

But who's paying the bill

For Keats and Shelley

Gerald Nicosia

Who rest beside you?

Ah, Gregory, I hope those

Small-time thugs who

Shake down the dead

Wake up some night

With the hot lead of your mind

Scalding their dreams

Giving them endless nightmares

And teaching them the biggest lesson of all

that only the truly

and forever dead

would dream of

digging up

someone who is still alive

underground.

POEM FOR STANLEY

who boxed, pitched, husked corn, rode the rails, and painted
"with kissing colors" according to his friend Jack Kerouac

Kerouac's pants no longer hang on your studio wall

the studio's no longer there

you had to sell them to build

a new studio at your wife's house

what a sacrifice that was!

you died climbing the rickety stairs

to the attic in her house

where you had to store all your unsold paintings

fell and broke all those 90-year-old bones

that didn't mend or got infected

who knows?

the doctors said the pain

was so bad

it was better you died

but Stan

I can still see you smiling and laughing

at all the fools who didn't understand

Kerouac and you and don't

understand art either

"Let's watch a baseball game on TV tonight!"
you told me—probably
the last thing you said to me
and I'll watch the Cubs
tonight in your honor
and laugh just like you at
all the fools who don't know
the game is won already
when we put a baseball
a brush, or a pen in our hand
and go to work
"I don't know what you do for a living,"
a guy once told you as
you stretched a canvas
"But whatever it is
you do it well"
and don't forget to press down tight
and flat against that jolting boxcar
as your train enters
the final
tunnel.

THE DISAPPEARING FOLKSINGER NON-BLUES

Steve Goodman came to visit me today

He had the same goofy grin

On his face that he wore all over Chicago

At his concerts

And getting high with his friends

While dodging Chicago's

Feel-good police and

Telling, as they said, the worst jokes

Ever heard

I remember him fast-moving in the flesh

In the lobby of the Evanston Holiday Inn

Barely glimpsed his face as he

Hurried by, guitar case slung at his side

Maybe a ghost already as Kerouac

Would have said

On his way to the stars

What a blessed man

And how blessed I was by his visit today

He belted music at me

Out of the blue

Out of the thin air

He ran me over with

"The City of New Orleans"

He told me everybody needs to live

As long as they possibly can

Because living on earth

Is the art of beating

The "disappearing railroad blues"

And beating any kind of disappearance

whatsoever

By finding your own immortality

You need to love life

He told me

Because it's gone

Soon enough

He touched me on the shoulder and

Then he left

And by God his visit

Was the realest thing in my day

And maybe the realest thing

I'll ever know.

POEM WRITTEN ON RICHARD BRAUTIGAN'S BIRTHDAY

What would Richard Brautigan say
about a Mill Valley café
on a cold January evening
filled with loud talk
and clinking dishes
old men conferring
and young couples flirting
would he say something
witty so you wouldn't know
how lonely he was
and still the outsider
at every festive gathering?
would he just sit silently
sipping his orange juice and vodka
and spinning the quarter he planned
to leave the pretty
red-haired waitress
as a tip and wondering
where happiness had gone?

Gerald Nicosia

what would Brautigan say
as the light grew dim outside
and one by one the patrons
left the café
to darkness and to him?
would he laugh softly to himself
at private literary jokes about
old morbid Thomas Gray and the loss
of his own clean,
well-lighted place
or would he
crumple the page in front of him
put his pen back in his pocket
and give it up for the night?
what would Richard Brautigan say
if he could see me here
48 years after his death
remembering him at not quite 50
wanting to go out the door
forever?
if he could have seen me
thinking about his suicide
on this cold January evening
far in the future

his 77th birthday
with him long in the earth
would it have stopped him
from doing it?
or would he have
smiled in amazement at a world
that never stops wanting
to kill itself?
maybe he'd just say
"Bring me my check
I have to go home now"—
secretly afraid
that there was actually
nowhere to go
even for the funniest man
on earth?

Gerald Nicosia

DADDIO PETE

My father was an angry man
Never stopped running from his angers
He was on a fast track
A treadmill
With angers always gaining on him
Making him breathe hard
Keeping his face red
Bald forehead bathed in sweat
And his grey-blue eyes
As my mom used to say
(almost always in fear of him)
Continually "turning white"
From the heat of his anger.
It was a terror to be around him
When the anger seized him
He was like a bull that saw red
And anything you said was a red flag
It seemed like I spent half my childhood
On the run from him
No matador was I
But a coward running for the stands

Anything to be out of reach of it

The worst part of course

Was he was goring himself constantly with it

He never seemed to know where it was coming from

Many times I didn't run fast enough

Didn't dodge well enough

We were both gored by it

I watched him die in my arms

Orange juice dribbling from his lips

On the kitchen floor

Where he'd fallen stone dead

That twenty-below winter night

The anger finally starting to cool

And condense into sorrow—

My own—

On his brow

Uniting us in that one moment

When anger's power

Could touch each of us

No longer.

Gerald Nicosia

POEM FOR TED BERRIGAN *(1934-1983)*

Hardly knowing me, Ted,

you talked my ear off about Kerouac and O'Hara

when I was a wide-eyed kid

hauling my recording junk several floors

up to your bedside

you gave me that sense of fire

that blew apart your best poems

and let a raw red Irish heart show through

brilliant as a Japanese setting sun

I heard the "gunfire inside your poems"

in every word you spoke

lying flat on your back in pain

on an unmade bed

in that dirty narrow apartment

which made me feel instantly at home

like the eternally messed-up house I grew up in

you were totally without pretension

and at the same time all pretension

but you put it all out on the platter for me

to see and eat

as if you were the Lower East Side's answer

to the Sacred Host—

while you guzzled colas and searched me

with your big bug eyes

all magnified by glasses that were like

some naturalist's lenses

and at the heart of the croak in your voice

I heard the unasked question—

the question you really wanted to ask

of everybody you met—

did we think you really made a difference

with your Life and Words?

the answer, Ted, is an unequivocal "Yes"

I should have told you then

but I was even shyer than you

I only wish you could have lived to hear it

I only wish you could have believed more

in the trees and flowers, however "shadowy,"

and the green peace at the heart of existence,

and less in the garbage cans and grimy sidewalks

and rush of honking ugly traffic

that dragged you to your death.

Gerald Nicosia

THE ATOM BOMB OF GENIUS

For Gregory Corso (1930-2001)

Gregory, everyone's got a memorial poem

for you.

I remember how cutting you could be—

you called one of my girl-friends a "cunt"—

you told Micheline, "I'm smarter

than you are, Jack."

"You've read more than me,"

Micheline said grudgingly,

taking the hit like a man.

Sometimes I wondered how so many people

could love you

as surely they did

but every so often just the sheer energy

you manifested

for days on end

with little sleep

would amaze me like the atom bomb

you wrote of so explosively

and I realized people had to acknowledge you

as a phenomenon of nature

if nothing else.

There will never be another Gregory Corso

or if there is,

he will spit on you,

the real Gregory Corso

to make way for himself

because the most outstanding thing about you

was your undaunted, unfazed,

unstoppable originality

it was what made you so mean

and terrible sometimes —

you couldn't let anything stand in the way

of your creativity

of creating a man/poet/

lover/child

messenger of the gods

like no one ever saw before

or since

and if we didn't love that,

you knew,

there was absolutely

no hope

for us.

Gerald Nicosia

MIDWEST RHAPSODY

I was born in Illinois
where the summer cicadas
set your teeth on edge
heavy clouds of wet air drifting
off the Mississippi made you sweat all night
the July sun burnt holes in my dreams
I wanted out and away
the big world that would eat me alive
Illinois was Hicksville
even Chicago seemed stuck in the corner
of a weedy cornfield
you can never escape the Midwest
it comes to me in dreams now
so many nights I can't get away
I'm back living in a small apartment with my mother
we're cold, we want to get back to California
we don't have any money
I look out the window in my dreams
it's always night and the snow is falling
Illinois is my home
no more and yet

I walk those tarry streets forever

in my mind, see the frustrated

yearning faces of people

who never quite made it

but were all on their way to somewhere else

little did they know it was

to become the angels

of my most potent

poignant memories.

Gerald Nicosia

FOR JOHN—NOW THAT HE IS NO MORE

in memoriam John Montgomery (1919-1992)

Good man, John, merry old Marin climber

took me by surprise with his

frontal assault on my ego

took my brain apart and

stored it in his private library

acted like he cared for nothing

and cared about us all

but couldn't show it

without a sneer or sly laugh

secret letter writer on midnight typewriter

spinning spider web of confidantes

throughout the world

tied together with the heart

of his friend Jack Kerouac

house musty with old books

always in need of companions

championing every lost cause

working for the post office and

spending half his earnings on postage

took literature seriously

never forgot the needy

insisted on a righteous country

or else he wanted no part

of the America that called him crazy

took pride in shocking the bourgeoisie

felt let down when no one called

will always be remembered

as the man you could talk to

when no one else was listening

by this one poet

he thought wasn't so bad

meaning me

now that he's no longer here

it's up to us to speak

as he did

and that means

tell the truth

for if we do

he'll live on in our heads

as he does now in our hearts

Adios, friend!

Gerald Nicosia

DEATH ROW PENNSYLVANIA

for Robert Lark and "the childred"

Sugar Bear, the weight of the world
is on the glass between us
the glass you lean against
ought to break
from the weight you carry
but prisons are built to keep
everything from breaking
except the people
inside them
Sugar Bear I want to sugarcoat your words
because they are so deliciously
full of life
I hope my children and
their children's children
will hear them in
the same excited tenor
you speak them in
before they try to stop you
With a needle full of poison
Sugar Bear they are poor men indeed

who need your death

to make them feel good

about anything

I know you have done things wrong

so have we all

but God above can forgive

and men have lost him utterly

when they are kept from doing the same

by the prison of their fears

and the execution of their dreams

of a world where a man can love

his fellow men

with the welcome of a smile

given freely

and nothing expected in return

but the courtesy of human dignity

as you love each one who comes to visit you

for two hours only

in Death Row Pennsylvania.

Gerald Nicosia

JULY VISIT WITH THE DEAD IN HILLSIDE, ILLINOIS

(half a year after my mother's death)

My mother and dad lie quietly here
in the humid summer stillness
as quietly as the world will let them
the birds still chirp and call
an occasional Fourth of July bomb
pops loud and angry
while planes cut in from time to time
even a helicopter *whacka-whacka-whack*-ing
and periodically the motor hum and rolling tires
of other living folk who've come
to visit the dead they loved
and still do love
the sky is darkening
ever so slowly
over the decades of work
my mother and father did upon this earth
to give me everything I needed
and still do need
to make my own work possible

and see me on my own hard journey

to just so quiet a place

I rest here with the dead

they comfort me

ask no favors

give no advice

demand no attention

they simply are at one at last

with earth and universe

and God who made us all

they promise justice in the end

for all our suffering

a home awaiting all our million steps

I share their home

for several precious minutes

just a guest for now

but someday here for good

born again by dying

into this one great family

of sorrowful Man

whose greatest hope

lies in the darkness

that will someday cover each of us

like a great woven blanket of care

Gerald Nicosia

Caw! Caw! Caw! Caw! Caw!

And when the crow stops crying

the wind makes magic soughing in the maple tree

raising the leaves before me

in miraculous greeting*

then one lone gull soars overhead

like my mother's soul set free

just so the dead still speak to us

though their human forms are gone.

*My grandmother Anna Ruzička Fremer always wanted to be buried under a maple tree.
She was. And a big one now stands across the road from my own mother Sylvia's grave.

ON PASSING THE CLOSED STOREFRONT OF ABANDONED PLANET BOOKSTORE ONE SATURDAY NIGHT

I glance into the dim window

of the closed bookshop

looking by habit for John Bryan

I'm tired—brain not fully working

I've forgotten for

an existential moment or two

that he's been dead half a year

my brain peers in

toward the comfortable swivel chair

the cluttered desk

the rows of long-out-of-print books

expecting to see his ruddy face

his marvelous fluff of white hair

like Villon's unmelted "snows of yesteryear"

his blue eyes filled with

ever-youthful, hard and angry

intelligence which

meeting mine

always melt into

a smile of hello

but tonight only emptiness and

dead and forgotten books

meet my gaze

books that like my jolted brain

the moment someone opens one

will be as alive as

my memories of John

his apartment is still there

on Brosnan Street

where he lived for 25 years

I can't pass that either

without thinking of him,

the printing press in his living room

or the stacks of freshly-printed papers

blocking the light

in his entryway

in bookstores like

the Abandoned Planet

you can buy someone else's memories

but we don't need a bookshop

to hold our own past because it's

with us all the time.

THE MAN WITH THE BIGGEST LAUGH
for Reginald Lockett

I remember many things about him
but nothing more strongly than
his laugh, the biggest laugh I
ever heard from anyone, man or woman
it started up slow like a
steam locomotive
and then got to chugging down
the track and kept on
chugging till everybody else was laughed
out and left way behind
Walter Mosley created a
great character called Easy Rawlins
and the moment I heard that name I
thought of Reggie 'cause
he was the easiest man I
ever knew—he made
living look easy
and laughing look easier
and writing look like eating
a big piece of pie

and you could just see him smacking

his lips when he read

a poem or a story he liked

that man loved living so much it

made you question why some people

don't but Reggie would

have been the first to forgive

anybody who didn't or who

maybe took a shortcut out

he sure didn't

he lived a full one

he's laughing now in heaven for sure

at the rest of us who

might think there was

something sad about his dying

when it was just his life getting to the brim and

couldn't get any fuller so

it spilled out onto

the page of all

those other lives around him

likes yours and mine

to make us that much richer

oh I should have said a

word too about his kindness 'cause

maybe that spilled over the brim even fuller

than his laughter

he had a kindness for everyone

and how can you not remember lovingly

a man like that?

requiescat in pace, Reggie,

and thanks for making

my life so much richer.

Gerald Nicosia

BOOK DEPOT CAFÉ IN EARLY OCTOBER

In the old railroad Depot building,

Now a bookstore café with

The crumbling stucco walls, flaking paint

And noisy pipes that let everyone

Know they can finally

Let their hair down

Mr. Homeless Crazy, bearded and bald who

Always looks dark and dirty

In standard garb of work pants and hooded sweatshirt

Sits hands clasped in front of him

Staring Zen-like over

His half-empty coffee cup

Two tables down from him

A loud con artist

Aggressively tries to sell his potential victim

A franchise of his "business"

Telling him how his London office

"Made a million dollars last year …

Though you might have to leave a little

Money on the table this year."

(Ha ha)

Assuring his would-be victim he'll be taking

Year-long sabbaticals soon enough

"Now if you say to yourself, 'Why am I

Taking this job?'" Mr. Aggressive asks,

And then spends the next half hour answering

Answering answering

While his potential victim nods

With eyes downcast

Two tables down from them, the same

Quiet blonde woman

With black roots showing proudly

Works quietly as she always does

On her laptop

Two tables down sit I, taking it

All in—wondering

Which of us is really holy?

Outside, the wind blows the leaves—

The first drops of rain.

Gerald Nicosia

THE MAN WHO STOPPED TO SAY HELLO

for Philip Lamantia (1927-2005)

Sweet Philip
you walked away from fame
when everyone else
was walking toward it
I remember the beautiful leather huaraches
you wore at your final reading
at City Lights
that looked like you could walk forever
in them
walking is how I'll always remember you
strolling one sunny Saturday past
the Savoy Tivoli
and Bob Kaufman calling to you
"Philip, come here!
There's a biographer who wants
to talk to you!"
the biographer was me
and you'd been avoiding my studied letters
but now it was different

I was the friend of a friend

you stopped to say hello

and talked to me for two straight hours

about Jack Kerouac

and Dore Schary

and the *Surrealist Manifesto*

I could have listened to you forever

and I understood why Jack

said you had the most magical voice of any man

he'd met

and finally you walked away,

such a happy smile on your face

the world was the biggest treat imaginable

to you

you had to keep walking

to savor it all

fame and money would have caused

intolerable delays

you sauntered like Thoreau

and Grant Avenue was

your Concord

your small apartment

on Filbert Street

made do as hermit's cabin

and every poem you wrote

as original as *Walden*

Thoreau avoided worldly success

just as you did

to be "captain of a huckleberry party"

And you were the captain

of all the North Beach poets

fueled by endless cappuccinos

and the dream of the unknown

you led us all to kinder realms

than the world underfoot

and the truth of that was in the fact

that you always had time

and disposition

to stop and say hello

when the heart was calling.

BEAT THE HEAT

for Bobby Waddell

Bobby Waddell stares
out of his small-town Arkansas jail
waiting extradition to California
and fifteen years behind bars
two strikes plus
"flight to avoid prosecution"
Bobby fucks them with
his blue eyes wide
open
Bobby still loves
this world
beat the heat, Bobby
for all of us!

Bobby Waddell came out of Arkansas
a long time ago
his father was a soldier
his stepfather a career
military man
Vietnam did a number on Bobby's head
a man in a wheelchair

taught him his own self-worth

Bobby ran the gamut from A to Z

from rich to poor

from lover to one who is destroyed

by hatred

it was a woman did him in

or maybe it was the war

or maybe it was just one blowjob too many

in a city parking lot at dusk

when all his best customers

stopped buying

what he was selling

and whisky and vodka didn't do it

any more

beat the heat, Bobby

beat the fucking heat

for all of us!

Bobby Waddell who hitchhiked across America

with the prettiest redheaded woman

in Indiana

fucked her on camera

so all his friends could see

how much he loved her

how beautiful they looked together

Bobby delivered his own baby

bathed his kid in a tub full of paralyzed vets

Bobby helped everybody in the whole

goddamn VA hospital

the Judge said

"I can't wipe out that other strike, son

I got to follow the law."

Bobby just looked at him and saw

a jackrabbit's tail disappearing in

the Arkansas brush

when he got out on bail

his lawyer threw up his hands and said

"He's in the wind now"

and walked away

while the cool wind blew at Bobby's heels

beat the heat, Bobby

beat the fucking heat

for all of us!

Bobby made one final mistake

he had to call the girlfriend who'd turned him in

the first time

he still loved her

he had to prove that trust

was still alive in the world

she'd let the guys in black

tap her phone

not two hours later

in the little Arkansas town where Bobby was born

the men in black surrounded

the little shack he'd holed up in

that was the end of Bobby Waddell's

life as a free man

the doctors gave his dying hep-C liver

three more years

the feds were giving him fifteen to life

that was the end of Bobby Waddell's

career as an activist

for peace and justice and

God help us, veterans' rights

it was just the beginning of Bobby's voice

coming down like thunder

on this fucked-up country

beat the heat, Bobby

beat the devil's heat forever

for all of us.

SEPTEMBER 19, 1996

87 years ago my baby father
squalls in Chicago—
eve of fall, his little Italian mother,
my grandmother, sighs
at end of labor pains
the future has given her a second son—
it will give her a 3rd son soon
and then a daughter
and then her husband will be shot dead
in a Taylor Street tavern
the week before Christmas, 1914—
and 87 years later I give that bright future
she lost
to my daughter Wu Ji,
born in Third World China
and brought to Marin County, California,
because I love her
and because this life

requires transformations

and because love triumphs

not in spite

but because

of them.

A POET'S GROCERY LIST

for Ted Joans (1928-2003)

Okapi, funky, cowries—
these are words Ted Joans taught
me and my mind
wanders to him as a wild deer in Marin
bounds at
almost African ancestral speed
across Blythedale
beating Ford's gas guzzlers by a mile
and I think how
Ted Joans had that
same ancestral African speed
as he bounded past all of us
on his romps through Beat, surrealist,
bebop jazz, and a
thousand other worlds
having the best damn time
of any writer in America
and if there was a dark side
and there was a dark side

keeping it as hidden as

some African tribal healer's darkest

secrets

for only the privileged few

Ted hands me a grocery receipt

from Albertson's

because he needs to give me

some information

and it's all he has in his pocket

to write on

but I wonder now if he

really wanted me to see

what he was living on

as I write the poem about

him he probably

knew I'd write

after he died

in

ALBERTSONS BONUS BUY PROGRAM

a lonely one-room apartment

in Vancouver

S & W BEANS

what kind of poet's feast is this?

YOU SAVED .59 ON BONUS BUYS

a poor man's feast, I think

I wonder if he even paid

with food stamps

this VIP, self-dubbed,

a Very Impecunious Poet

CANNED BEANS

I wish I'd taken him out

for a steak dinner

that night after his reading

at City Lights

when he tottered on frail,

rail-thin

shaky

legs

but his eyes still flashed with

angry humor

HOT SAUCE

he was living on beggar's food

eating what the homeless eat

wondering how long it would go on,

losing patience with people's

ignorance and folly

why only a handful knew what

a great poet

PINQUITOS

he really was

KIDNEY BEANS

he was Ted Joans, master

trickster, master con man, master clown

master human being

his head was a museum of

African lore straight from Harlem

and Harlem jive re-bongo-ized

by 30 winters in Timbuktu

Ted's beating heart

CHILI

taught me all I needed to learn

CANNED BEANS

about jazz

SARDINES

and about love

TAX .00

and about the poet's insatiable appetite

BALANCE 6.67

that can be fed for pennies

YOUR SAVINGS TODAY!

or just

BONUS BUY SAVINGS

a friendly smile

$2.35

of recognition

THANK YOU FOR SHOPPING

At Ted's

WE'RE DIMMING OUR LIGHTS FOR YOU!

Bon appetit

Theodorable

You.

SOCIAL JUSTICE 101

When I was ten
my father told me
everything I needed to know
was in a book by
Jack London
called *The Iron Heel*
but all he needed to know
about life
came from the Swede
who slurred him
because of his dark skin
and the German
who kicked his shoeshine box
into the street
in Hell's Half Acre
Taylor and Halsted
stiffing him for the shoeshine
laughing and calling
him "guinea and "wop"
while he looked in vain
for a brick to throw

at the vanishing racist

bastard

sometimes he'd quote me

lines from

that book about the

oppressed poor

who were his brothers even

though they were either

"blond beasts"

or pale-skinned, beat-down

factory workers with

Anglo-Saxon names

not a "dago" among them

it didn't matter

he understood being

on the wrong end

of a club or

a gun barrel

he was permanently awed

that someone could put

the life of endless

daily

urgent need

that seared his flesh

like a red-hot branding iron

into stone-cold, stone-hard

words that would last

a lot longer than

his or anyone's

perishable, oppressable

flesh

when he'd say the name

"Jack London"

there was a reverence in his voice

because truth-tellers

rated his highest

respect

and though the Bible

sat every day of his life

on his dresser

gathering dust

it was books like

The Iron Heel

which he never owned a copy of

that were his truest holy books

that he looked to for guidance

because

"Real life is the best teacher"

he'd say
and sometimes
when he said it
he had to look away
because his eyes
were filled
with tears.

Gerald Nicosia

ZAKE

for Paulette Williams who became Ntozake Shange

Zake, I knew you were fragile

The first time I laid eyes on you

It was a reading at the Art Institute in San Francisco

With Jessica Hagedorn

And you were advertised as "the famous one"

But Jessica came forth two guns blazing

A knife's edge in her voice

That scared half the men in the room

Into covering their crotch

But you, Zake, read with great poise, fast, never tripping

On your exquisite stream of words

I could see you were a polished performer

But in your voice I heard something different

A soul's vulnerability and deep pain

You read about the black children disappearing in Atlanta

And it was as if it was your own child

Who had disappeared, been murdered

Many people saw only your fame

I saw a soul bared for the world

But I was too young myself then

To understand what such nakedness

Would cost you

Our friendship started more than a decade later

When I sat next to you at a reading upstairs in City Lights

And couldn't believe you had no one

To drive you home

And so I offered and felt again the immediacy

Of your open, glad heart

When friendship was handed to you

You had that shy look of

Someone who is always out of place

In a society that is above and beyond them

I saw your tentative moves and reach

Toward a world that too often

Turns out to be hostile

And I knew we were very much alike

The first party I took you to

You sat in a corner dressed in gorgeous bright colors,
    shining jewelry

Ruffles and flounces of every sort

And I wanted to protect you because

You looked like a delicate flower

That even too strong a wind

Could knock over or destroy

But always from within there welled up

That colorless and exceedingly hot flame

That burned its own indomitable path across the globe

That the powerful could only bow in awe of

And the poor and humble crowded close to

To warm their own flawed flesh

Zake, you were a hero to all who suffered or were oppressed

A hero in spite of yourself

I know you'd have chosen any other path

But it chose you

This world that won't let black folks alone

Had a special grudge for you with

Your proud and deadly words

You took all the medicines you could find

To ease your pain, legal

Or not

And the payback caught up with you too fast

But you refused to die, you lived on buffalo wings

Tequila, and 3 packs of cigarettes

A day longer than anyone

Would have bet on

Your head was a jukebox of every

Blues and jazz, salsa and doo-wop song ever written

I can still hear your wild laugh when

You raised people's eyebrows with sassy talk

Of your famous pussy posse

You were a character, a card, an American original

Broken free of the chains of slavery

And leading the pack of lonely geniuses

Of unfettered imagination

You were burdened with the weight of all the needy

But you loved life's games

You were merry with the madness of it all

You had more enthusiasm and hunger

For the next minute

Than anyone I ever met—

There's no one I'd rather spend a quiet hour with

No one I'd rather hear a new story from

Or an old memory

And you remembered everything

Your memory second only to

Your limitless kindness

I remember you in a hospital bed in Brooklyn

I brought you coffee and chocolate cake

And caught you making your nurses laugh

With bawdy tales of your own body

Molly Brown might have been Unsinkable

But you were Unshockable

You were working almost till the last minute

Till the last ounce of sacred Zake fuel

Had burned up in an all-out effort

To lead us

Out of darkness

And onto a solid path

That unlike your frail body

Could not be taken away.

THE BEAUTIES OF MY GENERATION

for Janine Pommy Vega (and with apologies to Stephen Spender)

I think continually of the beauties of my generation

naked rainbow-hued young bodies on the streets of San Francisco

or half a million unshorn children on the fields of Woodstock

unclothed in the rain, kissing

because it felt good, like pot, like acid,

like unmutilated flesh and breaking the law,

like spelling FUCK at the top of your lungs because Country Joe,

that excellent-hearted gentleman,

asked you to.

"Why not?" quoth Dayton Allen

a decade earlier on the safe and civil *Steve Allen Show*

not knowing how absolutely

bananas gonzo buggy trippy zapped and zonked lit-up burnt-out

freaking raving mad we'd all go with a few deranged

    cerebral molecules

and one of the cruelest, bloodiest wars in history

who could have dreamed it would have led to

Crosby Stills and Nash

like handsome young lieutenants serenading the troops
    of waywardness
for the sacred honor of "Judy Blue Eyes"?
I tell you I have seen sights that will last me a lifetime
the love so brilliant and hot it welded to my retinas
visions of giving and caring and goofing under the stars
while naming the constellations and rapping about
the hundred-and-one kama sutra ways to
leave the flesh behind
feed our heads and free ourselves
or of farmhouse nights drinking musty home-made wine
like grown-up children's grape juice
and reciting poetry to each other
our own words that no one could touch
least of all the war machine, the government, the cocksuckers
who wanted it all bought and sold and rendered into lard to clog
the arteries of dying America and hasten the corpse
for the guaranteed thousand-percent profit
of the dozen biggest corporate undertakers
O Neil Young we all sure as hell were baptized in a
    "Sea of Madness"
but we gave back more than we got
gave a whole nation new dreams, turned old men to children
and made old women glad, as the saying goes—

gave the earth a fresh spin, though no one knew toward what—

you can bet your last Richie Havens record we didn't intend

Ronald Reagan playing cowboys and Indians with the

    idiot plan

of filling all those reservations

now that the oil's depleted

with Russkies and maybe Sandinistas too

like everyone else on this planet we were powerless against time,

but somewhere out in space all those light rays from the glitter

of Janis's jewelry and Cassady's flying hammer

and the blinding strobes and the psychedelic color shows

and Kesey's many flags

are still illuminating the gods and ghosts who've made it home free

to that astral playland

where dead gurus still listen to the Beatles chanting mantras

and Bobby Kennedy's blue eyes are as silent as his brother John's

    were laughing

and Jimmy Hendrix takes one last energetic leap

over the rainbow of eternity

in the form of a dancing dolphin.

ABOUT THE AUTHOR

Born and educated in Chicago, Gerald Nicosia has spent the past forty years on the West Coast, mainly in the Bay Area. Best known for two large nonfiction works, *Memory Babe: A Critical Biography of Jack Kerouac* and *Home to War: A History of the Vietnam Veterans' Movement*, he has also worked extensively as a journalist, poet, and organizer of literary events. His biography of Kerouac, *Memory Babe*, which first came out in 1983 with Grove Press, will soon be published in a fourth, updated and revised edition; and it has been translated into several languages, mostly recently into Mandarin, in Shanghai, China.

Having moved to San Francisco in 1979, Nicosia became part of the post-Beat circle of poets in the Bay Area, and eventually numbered many of the Beat poets, including Jack Micheline, Harold Norse, Gregory Corso, David Meltzer, Jerry Kamstra, Howard Hart, Joanna McClure, Lenore Kandel, and Janine Pommy Vega among his good friends. He would also edit poetry collections by two of those friends, *Cranial Guitar* (1996) by Bob Kaufman and *Teducation* (1999) by Ted Joans. Beginning with *Lunatics, Lovers, Poets, Vets & Bargirls* (1991), he also began publishing books of his own poetry, of which *Beat Scrapbook* is number six. His poetry collection *Night Train to Shanghai* was widely praised, and *Huffington Post* reviewer Lionel Rolfe wrote that Nicosia "is a real poet, very much in the San Francisco tradition of Ferlinghetti, Patchen, Rexroth and Ginsberg." Rolfe compared *Night Train to Shanghai* to Blake's poem about America and said the book was "maybe even a great volume of poetry." Nicosia also organized and took part in hundreds of public poetry readings, for which he often worked with the San Francisco

Public Library and other Bay Area venues like the Unitarian Church, the Jewish Community Center, and Cloud House.

Nicosia has read his poetry throughout the United States and abroad, at such notable sites as Bob Holman's Bowery Poetry Club in New York, Bob Weir's Sweetwater Music Hall in Mill Valley, California, the Dylan Thomas Centre in Swansea, Wales, and Shakespeare & Company Bookstore in Paris. He was a close friend of the late poet and playwright Ntozake Shange and is currently working on a full critical biography of her.

In 2013, Nicosia received one of the first Acker Awards "for avant-garde excellence." He lives in Marin County, California.